Looking at
Small Mammals

Rodents

Sally Morgan

Chrysalis Education

Distributed in the United States by
Smart Apple Media
2140 Howard Drive West
North Mankato, Minnesota 56003

Text copyright © Sally Morgan 2004

Library of Congress Control Number 2004043801

ISBN 1-59389-177-6

Editorial Manager: Joyce Bentley
Series editor: Debbie Foy
Editors: Clare Lewis, Joseph Fullman
Designer: Wladek Szechter
Picture researcher: Sally Morgan
Illustrations: Woody

Picture acknowledgements:
Ecoscene: 21T Ian Beames, 13T, 17B, 18B Frank Blackburn,
4, 10, 11T Peter Cairns,
15B Papilio/Brian Cushing, 26 Michael Gore, 14, 27 Angela
Hampton, 20 Don Lester,
2 Neeraj Mishra, 5T Robert Nichol, 16 Papilio/Steve
Austin, 1, 12 Papilio/Clive Druett, 5B Papilio/William
Dunn, 3B Papilio/Jamie Harron,11B Papilio/Jack
Milchanowski, 7B,15T, 21B, 32 Papilio/Robert Pickett, 3T,
7T, 8, 9T, 13B, 17T, 18T, 19, 22, 23T, 23B, 24, 25T, 25B
Robin Redfern, 9B Visual & Written. Front cover: TR
Frank Blackburn, B Neeraj Mishra, TCL, TL Papilio/Clive
Druett, TCR Papilio/Robert Pickett, CR, CL Robin
Redfern. Back Cover: TR Frank Blackburn, TCL,TL
Papilio/Clive Druett, TCR Papilio/Robert Pickett,
Holt Studios: 6 Nigel Cattlin.

Printed in China

Contents

What are rodents?

Rodents belong to a group of animals called **mammals.** Most mammals have four legs and are covered in hair. They give birth to live young.

Rodents, such as this red squirrel, are covered in thick fur.

Marmots can survive the cold winter weather of mountain regions.

Young mammals feed on their mother's milk for the first months of their lives. Rats, mice, and guinea pigs are all rodents. The word *rodent* means to **gnaw**.

A tiny harvest mouse climbs over a seed head looking for seeds to eat.

The rodent family

Most rodents are small animals with long tails. Their toes end in claws. Rodents have very large front teeth called **incisors**. They use their incisors to gnaw and scrape their food. They also gnaw on wood, electric cables, wires, and plastic.

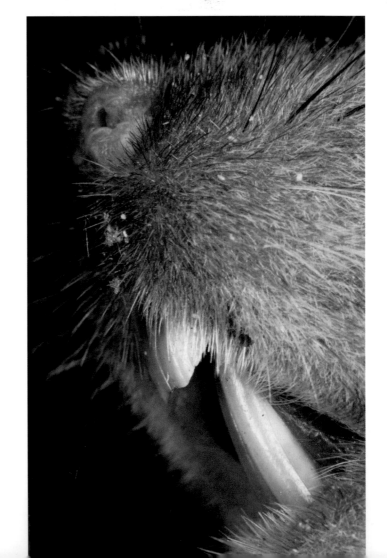

The sharp incisors of a rat are good for gnawing food.

6

Mice use their long tails to balance as they climb.

Rodents' incisors never stop growing and always stay sharp.

The groundhog's feet have toes that end in claws.

Where do rodents live?

Rodents are found all over the world. In fact, there are very few places where you do not find them!

They are found in many different types of habitat.

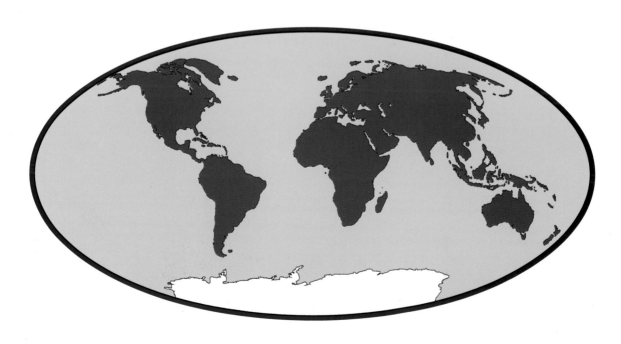

The areas shaded in pink on this map of the world show where rodents live.

The rat is found in towns and cities, fields, and farms.

They live in rain forests, woodlands, grasslands, deserts, and the frozen Arctic. Some rodents have moved into towns and cities. Some may even live in our homes!

The Arctic ground squirrel is found in the Far North, where the ground is frozen for much of the year.

The water vole lives along streams and rivers.

The squirrels

The thick, bushy tail of the gray squirrel helps it to balance as it climbs trees.

There are many different types of squirrels, for instance, red and gray squirrels, beavers, prairie dogs, and marmots. Most squirrels have a slender body and a long, bushy tail. Squirrels are good at climbing.

They can run up tree trunks and jump from branch to branch. Prairie dogs like to dig.

They build a **maze** of tunnels where they can hide when danger threatens.

Prairie dogs live together in underground tunnels.

11

The mouse family

Mice have a pointed face with long **whiskers** around their nose. Their eyes look like bright, black beads. Most mice are **nocturnal**. This mean they come out to feed at night.

The spiny mouse has long whiskers to help it "feel" its surroundings.

Harvest mice climb to the top of cereal plants to find the seeds.

Mice use their sense of smell and hearing to find their way around in the dark. The mouse family includes mice, rats, hamsters, voles, and lemmings. They live in many different types of habitat. The jerboa lives in deserts, and the naked mole-rat lives in **burrows** underground.

The edible dormouse lives in trees where it searches for fruit.

The guinea pigs

Guinea pigs belong to a group of rodents called cavies. Other cavies include the porcupine, chinchilla, and agouti. Cavies are larger than the other rodents.

Guinea pigs have plump bodies and short legs.

Agoutis are always listening for the sound of fruit (their favorite food) hitting the ground.

Cavies have large heads and sturdy bodies. Some have a short tail and others have no tail at all. Cavies are noisy. They make a variety of sounds including chirps, squeaks, and burbles.

The body of the porcupine is covered in long spines and quills. When it is threatened, a porcupine raises its quills and stamps its feet.

15

What do rodents eat?

Most rodents eat plant foods, such as leaves, fruits, seeds, and roots. Some rodents are **omnivorous**. This means they feed on both plant and animal foods.

This bank vole is gnawing on a nut with its incisors.

Field voles are herbivores. They feed mostly on leaves.

For instance, the spiny mouse eats seeds and grass, but it also **preys** on insects. Water rats eat snails. Some rodents store food in the summer and fall to eat during the cold winter months.

Squirrels feed on nuts, seeds, and fruits. Sometimes they eat insects.

This edible dormouse smells a nut that it has found in a tree.

Finding food

Rodents have particularly good senses of smell, hearing, and touch. They use these senses to find food.

The wood mouse has long whiskers at both sides of its nose.

Rodents can hear sounds that people cannot. Their whiskers are sensitive to touch. Nocturnal rodents have large eyes to help them see in the dark.

A rat stands up on its back legs and sniffs the air. This helps the rat to find food.

19

Getting around

The squirrel's tail grips a pole as it tries to steal some nuts from a bird feeder.

Rodents can run fast along the ground. Rats and mice can climb up ropes and the walls of buildings. Squirrels can climb up and down trees.

They use their long, bushy tail for balance as they leap from branch to branch.

The flying giant squirrel has a flap of skin between its arms and legs. This is like a wing to help the squirrel glide. Some rodents, such as beavers and rats, can swim.

Rodents as pests

Mice and rats can be found in towns and cities, where they live in and under buildings. They feed on piles of garbage they find in the streets. These rodents breed very quickly.

Rats can squeeze through small gaps in walls and floors.

*House mice come
out at night to feed
on leftover food.*

In a short time, a few rats or mice can become many. In some places, they are **pests** because there are too many of them. They damage food stores and carry diseases.

*Mice may chew
through electric cables
and damage wiring.*

These baby mice are only three days old. They are pink and have no fur.

Life cycle

Rodents only live for a few years. Some of the smaller rodents can breed when they are just a month or so old. A female mouse and rat can have several **litters** of babies every year. There are from five to ten babies in a litter. A

These baby rats are 21 days old and they are ready to explore their surroundings.

vole can have as many as 13 litters in a year.

Baby rodents are born without any hair. They are small and pink, and stay in their nest to keep warm. They feed on their mother's milk. In a few weeks, they will be large enough to leave the nest and explore.

By the time they are 13 days old, baby mice have fur but are not yet ready to leave the nest.

25

Big relatives

Most rodents are small animals, but there are a few large rodents. The capybara is the largest.

Capybaras are herbivores. They live next to water and feed on grasses.

The mara has long legs and can run up to 28 miles (45 kilometers) per hour.

The capybara looks like a giant guinea pig, with a large head and square body. It swims in rivers and lakes. The agile mara is another large rodent. It has long legs and looks like a small deer. It can run quickly and jump.

Investigate!

Urban rodents

Rodents can be seen in backyards and parks, and even on some city streets. Look for squirrels visiting bird tables to steal the seeds and nuts. They are like acrobats as they climb up fences, trees, and bird tables. They can even run across washing lines!

Squirrels are regular visitors to bird tables and feeders.

Pet rodents

Rodents such as gerbils, mice, hamsters, chinchillas, and rats are popular pets. You can learn a lot about rodents from observing their behavior. Watch how they eat their food. You may be able to see some of the large rodents, such as beavers, maras, and capybaras, in zoos and wildlife centers. Find out more about rodents by reading books and searching the Internet.

Many people keep small rodents as pets, especially mice, gerbils, and hamsters.

Nature detective

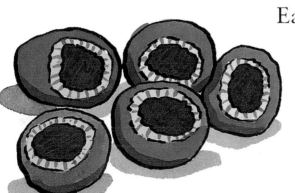

Squirrels, mice, and voles eat nuts and pine cones. Each rodent eats the food in a different way. By looking at the remains of a nut or a pine cone, you can tell what type of rodent ate it.

The way these hazelnuts have been eaten is a clue that they were eaten by a bank vole.

Rodent facts

✓ Naked mole-rats live underground in tunnels. They form "digging chains," or chains of mole-rats lined up head to tail, who tunnel and find food.

✓ The giant flying squirrel can glide over 400 yards (400 meters) as it leaps from a tall tree to a lower tree.

✓ The beaver can fell trees by chewing through the wood near the ground. It uses tree trunks to build dams across rivers.

✓ The black-tailed prairie dogs live together in a network of underground burrows called towns.

These silhouettes show the size of a mara and a rat compared to the size of a human foot.

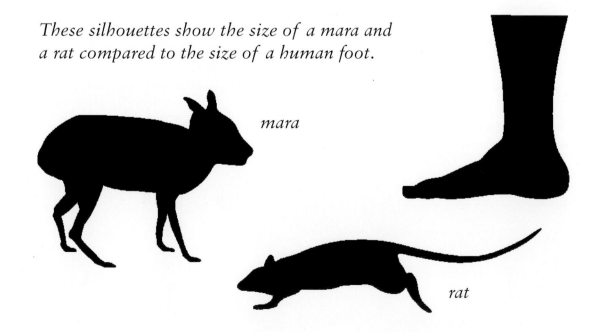

mara

rat

Glossary

burrow A large hole or tunnel in the ground.

gnaw To scrape or chew on food.

incisor A tooth at the front of the mouth.

litter Baby animals born at the same time to the same mother.

mammal An animal that feeds its young with milk and is covered in fur.

maze A complex network of passages.

nocturnal Active at night, asleep during the day.

omnivorous Eating both plant and animal foods.

pest An animal that is destructive, that destroys crops, damages buildings, or carries disease.

prey (on) To hunt another animal for food.

whisker Stiff hair found around the mouth and nose of a mammal that is sensitive to touch.

Index